Rabbits
as a Hobby

BOB BENNETT

SAVE-OUR-PLANET SERIES

T.F.H. Publications, Inc.
1 T.F.H. Plaza • Third & Union Aves. • Neptune, NJ 07753

Table of Contents

Photography:
H. Bielfeld,
Bruce Crook,
Marvin
Cummings,
Michael Gilroy,
R. Hanson,
Burkhard Kahl,
H. Reinhard,
M.F. Roberts,
D. Robinson,
and Vincent
Serbin.

Table of Contents

This book is dedicated to John for more than one reason.

Special thanks for help with the concept of this book go to Evelyn Axelrod.

Originally published as *The T.F.H. Book of Pet Rabbits,* 1982.

A Blue
Silver
Marten.

Large or small, rabbits are undeniably appealing creatures that can make wonderful pets.

Bob Bennett's involvement with rabbits is broad and deep. He began to raise them in Vermont in 1948 as a Boy Scout in pursuit of a merit badge. Twenty-five years later he wrote a new merit badge manual for the Boy Scouts of America, *Raising Rabbits*. It is currently in use, with requirements that he devised for the badge.

In 1971 he founded *Domestic Rabbits* magazine and served as its first

The author and his daughter Alyssa admiring "Dimes," Alyssa's Black Dutch. Notice the manner in which the rabbit is being held: firmly supported under the rump.

editor. In 1975 he became rabbit editor of *Countryside* magazine and in 1977 became technical editor of a new magazine called *Rabbits* about raising rabbits. It was in 1975 that *Raising Rabbits the Modern Way* was published. In 1977 his book on rabbit shows, *Bob Bennett's Guide to Winning Rabbit Shows*, was published. In 1984 his Raising Rabbits Successfully, a new and comprehensive manual, was published. Since 1983 he has edited *Buck and Doe*, a newsletter for rabbit raisers.

Bennett has been active for many years in the American Rabbit Breeders Association. In 1976 he was elected a director of the association. He has served as president of the American Tan Rabbit Specialty Club.

Bob Bennett is perhaps best known to serious rabbit fanciers as the breeder and exhibitor of his "Famous Tans," a name the rabbits received after being

A Britannia Petite. This is one of the smallest breeds of rabbit.

A Himalayan. As a Himalayan ages, the color of its nose, ears, feet, and tail may fade somewhat.

About the Author

A Checkered Giant. This is a large breed of rabbit whose weight averages 12 pounds or more.

written up widely in the United States and Europe. His Tans gave him his biggest thrill when he won Best of Breed and best of three of the four colors of Tans at the 1975 ARBA Convention. He now lives in Vermont, where he raises rabbits on ten acres overlooking Lake Champlain and the Adirondack and Green Mountains.

Introduction

A small wire carrying cage with a metal tray under its all-wire floor makes for safe and convenient transportation. The author's daughter Alyssa takes her pet to rabbit shows in this carrier.

I wish you had bought this book before you brought home your pet rabbit. At least, I hope you get it at the same time. If not, very soon after.

That's because you have taken responsibility for a live animal. If it's caged, as it probably is most of the time, it is totally dependent upon you. And if it is loose in your yard it is still almost as dependent, because your rabbit is a domesticated animal, not a wild one. It does not have the keen instinct and defenses of a wild rabbit. It does not have a sense of fear resulting from experiences in the wild. And it probably can't run or hop as fast as its wild cousin.

Your first responsibility is to feed this rabbit cor-

Baby Netherland Dwarfs, all under five months old.

rectly—to nourish what is probably a young and growing animal. If you read this book *before* you acquire a rabbit, this pet of yours will enjoy a proper diet from his first day in your care. Your second responsibility is to house your pet comfortably and safely.

You might read this book first and have the proper food and housing awaiting his arrival. Or your rabbit may right now be in a cardboard box in the garage or basement, nibbling lettuce or cabbage. If that's the case, the first thing you should do is take away the greens. Then provide a non-tipping dish of fresh clean water and, if you have no real rabbit pellets yet, a dish of dry oatmeal, and perhaps some dry bread. Make sure the box your rabbit is in has some holes for ventilation. Bedding the floor with straw, shavings or even torn strips of crumpled newspaper will keep him dry and comfortable for a day. Make sure no dogs or cats can get at him. Now he's okay until tomorrow. So take time out and read this book now. Your rabbit's life may depend upon it. You have taken on a weighty responsibility, and that's good. It is, in fact, an awful lot of what having a pet rabbit— or any pet at all— is about.

Close-up view of eight-day-old rabbits of one of the lop-eared breeds. Note how the ears are naturally folded down.

A red-eyed Netherland Dwarf doe.

The Rabbit as a Pet

Does a rabbit make a good pet? Why have one for a pet? What are the advantages? The disadvantages?

These are good questions that you might logically ask. Good, sound answers may help you decide whether to have a pet rabbit.

More often than not, however, you are likely to simply fall in love with a rabbit, perhaps one in a pet store window. Without thinking about the pros and cons, you are illogically, perhaps, captivated by this soft, fuzzy, furry, wiggly-nosed and cuddly creature.

Nevertheless, let's consider the attributes of the pet rabbit.

Rabbits do respond to your attention and like to be picked up and handled.

Some people say everything is "compared to what." If you will consider the rabbit as a pet, you might compare it to other animals. Let's compare it to man's best friend, the dog.

Compared to dogs, rabbits generally are not as affectionate, and they usually can't stand up to dogs in the tricks department. They can't pull your wagon, and they won't bark if a burglar breaks in. And, let's face it, they really are not as smart.

On the other hand, they don't make noise at any time; they never bark in the middle of the night to disturb family or neighbors. And they do respond to your care. Your rabbit will be glad to see you; it can show some affection. A rabbit can be taught a few tricks, as you will soon see. A caged rabbit always stays home in his own yard. He doesn't jump on visitors or trample the flowers. His droppings, or manure, are not found on sidewalk or lawn; in fact, they are not objectionable at all, appearing in the form of hard little balls, known affectionately as rabbit "raisins." Rabbit droppings are welcomed by gardeners of

Many people opt for a rabbit as their pet of choice because rabbits are quiet, clean, and require less care than other kinds of animals.

12

flowers, vegetables, trees and shrubs, as they have high fertilizer value compared to farm manures and, in addition, will not "burn" plants when applied without aging.

A rabbit is no real substitute for a dog, particularly when it comes to companionship, such as a walk in the woods on a snowy evening or chasing a stick in the surf on the beach. But a rabbit is easier to manage and can be kept in places where certain large dogs cannot.

13

A Sable Marten Netherland Dwarf. The average weight of adults of this breed is two pounds.

Compared to cats, rabbits usually are more dependably affectionate. Kept in a cage, they are more controllable and won't scratch the furniture or eat the houseplants. Of course, rabbits generally are not housepets, as are cats and dogs, and thus while they do not offer constant companionship, they also are not constantly underfoot as are some canines and felines.

As a caged animal, primarily, the rabbit perhaps is best compared to hamsters, gerbils, mice and guinea pigs. Because a rabbit is larger, it lends itself to more in the way of petting and snuggling. It has a longer life expectancy —eight to ten years or even more in some cases.

As for care, rabbits need less than dogs and cats and no more than much smaller caged animals. For example, they groom themselves much as do cats, and baths are not necessary. Bathing a dog can be a chore; professional grooming can be expensive. Rabbits need none of that.

Rabbits enjoy being picked up properly and petted. You will make your rabbit *your pet* by daily petting and occasional brushing. It won't require a great deal of effort on your part, but it should be regular and continual if you want your animal to be your friend.

One other consideration when deciding about a rabbit pet: remember, a domesticated rabbit is in an entirely different cate-gory when compared to dogs and cats as housepets and to mice, gerbils and hamsters as small caged mammals. A rabbit essentially is a farm animal. The great numbers of rabbits that exist today owe their lives to this fact. Rabbit farmers, large and small, breed rabbits primarily for their use as good nutritious meat—and also to serve science in the testing laboratories for the betterment of the lives of humans. Additional use is made of rabbit fur. Look around your house and you may find a garment with some rabbit fur, perhaps on collars or cuffs or hats. Did you know that real felt hats are made of rabbit fur? And that Thomas Alva Edison, who invented the light bulb and movies among other things, also invented felt? So a rabbit pet is a real farm animal pet, and perhaps this gives him a bit of distinction in the pet world.

HOW POPULAR ARE RABBITS?

Nobody knows exactly how many people are raising rabbits, but we can make some good guesses. The feed manufacturers, those companies that produce rabbit pellets, know how much feed they make and sell in a year. And they know how much

For optimum development, a young rabbit should spend the first eight weeks of its life with its mother.

A Black Dutch enjoying the comfort of a soft bed. Allowing your pet up on your furniture is a matter of personal choice.

feed each rabbit is likely to eat annually. Their guess is that more than 12 million rabbits are raised in the United States each year. And the largest of these feed companies recently reported that rabbit feed sales are increasing at a faster pace than sales of any other small animal feed. These companies have known for years that England, Italy, Germany, France and Spain produce far more rabbits than the United States. The Chinese also raise many rabbits, and rabbits are becoming more popular in South and Central America and in Africa.

So there are a lot of rabbits out there. But who is raising them? In the United States, more than 50,000 men, women and children are members of the American Rabbit Breeders Association Inc. Each of these members, almost without exception (you don't have to own even one rabbit to be a member), is a rabbit raiser. Several decades ago, when the ARBA membership rolls listed only about 7,000, the U.S. Census Bureau counted 250,000 house-holds with breeding rabbits—that's more than just one pet rabbit. So it's safe to say that the number of U.S. rabbit raisers is at least in the hundreds of thousands.

Most of them, of course,

do not raise thousands of rabbits but only dozens, or perhaps hundreds, each year. Most of the rabbit raisers do not live on farms, either, but raise these small farm animals in backyards, sheds, garages and even basements in our towns and cities. If you found your rabbit in a pet shop, the

Alyssa Bennett enjoying a quiet moment with Dimes. The more time you spend with your pet, the more he will grow accustomed to your company.

chances are that he arrived there from a small rabbitry, which is what we call a rabbit farm, right in a backyard in your own home town.

It is also probable that your local pet shop has rabbits on display, perhaps even in the window, only in the early spring, right around Easter. That's when most people get interested in rabbits. But if you want a rabbit at any other time of year and don't see any in the store, simply ask the manager if he can get you one. It's a good bet he will contact one of his Easter suppliers, a breeder who raises rabbits all year 'round.

So, one way or another, at any time of the year, you will be able to obtain a pet rabbit. But there are many different kinds in many different colors and sizes and shapes. Which is the right rabbit for you?

The Opal Netherland Dwarf exhibits the large head and eyes and short ears characteristic of its breed.

Choosing a Pet Rabbit

There are more than 40 breeds of rabbit—and more being developed all the time.

The rabbit you choose should be alert and interested in its surroundings.

Rabbits are hardy animals that can do well in captivity.

If you have simply fallen in love with a rabbit in the pet shop window, the answer to the question about choosing the right rabbit is easy. But if you are going about selecting a pet rabbit in a more rational way, there are several considerations to help you choose. These considerations can make a difference, not only in how your rabbit looks but also in how much he will eat and how big a cage, or hutch, as they are called, he will need—also, how easy or difficult he will be to lift and carry around. Even his personality, disposition and appetite for affection should be considered. Here's just one example: a full-grown adult rabbit, which yours will be in no more than three to four months after you receive him, can weigh anywhere from only two pounds (guinea pig size) to more than twenty pounds or as large as many breeds of small dogs. Your feed bill could be ten times larger with a giant rabbit than with a dwarf.

Chances are you will be buying a rabbit that is only two to three months old. Most rabbits are weaned (taken from the mother) at two months, and many states have laws that prohibit the sale of pet rabbits any younger. While it is entirely possible to take a baby rabbit from its mother at only three to four weeks and have it survive, it certainly is not in the best interests of the baby. Young rabbits need their mother's milk, or a scientifically formulated replacement, for at least another two to three weeks; a total of eight weeks with the mother is best for optimum early growth and development.

Most likely you will not be seeing the baby rabbit's parents. If you did, you would get a good idea of how big the baby will be. You might ask the sales clerk or manager if he knows what breed these rabbits are; if you know the breed, you could easily use information in this book to help you make a decision.

Don't be hasty in making your final selection. The more you know about the particular rabbit breed that interests you the better you will be able to determine whether it is the right breed for you.

The following information and the photographs in this book should go a long way in determining what sort of rabbit will be your pet.

In the United States and Canada, members of the American Rabbit Breeders Association have developed or recognized over 40 individual and distinct *breeds* of rabbits. Within many of these breeds are several *varieties*, which are distinguished by different colors or even patterns.

There are, for example, nine varieties of the Satin breed, fourteen varieties of the Rex breed and over thirty varieties of the Netherland Dwarf breed, the last resembling many of the larger breeds in color and markings. But let's back up a bit in describing rabbits so that we will really know what we are talking about, because *varieties* are near the tail end of the description.

An outstanding feature of the Lop breeds is their extremely long, floppy ears.

Always buy the best animal you can afford. A healthy rabbit is much easier to care for than one that is ill.

We know, of course, that rabbits are members of the animal kingdom and have been around for at least three and a half million years. Their footprints have been found in Africa in fossilized lava dust among those of the earliest hominids, or ancestors of modern man. Mary Leakey, wife of the late and famous Louis Leakey, perhaps the world's best-known anthropologist, reported this fact only in 1979. Rabbits have backbones and therefore are vertebrates. They are classed as mammals because they have hair or fur, suckle their live-born offspring, have a four-chambered heart and are warm-blooded.

Rabbits aren't rodents; they are lagomorphs. They belong to the order Lagomorpha, which comprises the pikas as well as rabbits and hares. Hares, by the way, are different from rabbits in that their young are born already furred (baby rabbits are born naked) and that adult hares are only wild, or undomesticated. The Belgian Hare, which is domesticated, is not a hare, but a rabbit. Rabbits belong to the family Leporidae, of which hares are the only other members. Their genus is *Oryctolagus* (European rabbit), and the species is *cuniculus*, derived from the Latin word that denotes wild rabbits'

and or Dutch, and the varieties, such as New Zealand White or Chocolate Dutch. Finally, there are the crossbred, or mongrel, rabbits whose ancestry includes two or more of the recognized breeds and whose appearance may be that of one of these breeds or something the likes of which has never been seen before and may never be seen again.

When you run into crossbreeds, you enter the arena of the unknown, because rabbits of different sizes can and do mate, producing offspring whose eventual size can only be the object of speculation.

habit of burrowing and that has given rise to the name given to rabbits in various languages. For example, the rabbit is *coniglio* in Italian, *conejo* in Spanish and *coney* in non-current English. Some furriers still describe rabbit fur with the word "coney."

Now that we know in general what a domesticated rabbit is, we get into the practical consideration of breeds, such as New Zeal-

Rabbits' capacity to multiply makes them easy to breed and raise.

Let's categorize the domestic rabbit by weight and by fur structure and then list the breeds and varieties you are likely to run across. This information, coupled with the photos in this book, should allow you to evaluate those rabbits in the pet store, even if the store personnel aren't quite sure what they are selling. You will also be able to ask for and describe what you want if the store doesn't have them in stock. You may even, with some imagination and a little luck, determine the ancestry and the eventual size and weight of crossbred rabbits. At least you will know that's what they

Within many of the rabbit breeds are many different color varieties.

are, for they will not match up to any description found in this book.

SIZES

The Biggest

The largest rabbits are called the giants. The Flemish Giant reputedly is the world's largest rabbit. When fully grown it weighs at least twelve or thirteen pounds, and some individuals have attained weights exceeding twenty pounds. Others are the Giant Chinchilla and the Checkered Giant. These rabbits can reach thirteen to sixteen pounds. When weaned they weigh about five pounds.

The Middleweights

Medium-weight rabbits reach nine to twelve pounds at maturity. About half of the recognized breeds fall into this category; they are produced in great numbers because they are the best size for a meat rabbit. When weaned, they weigh about four pounds. Included among them are the New Zealand, the Satins, the French and English Lops, the Rex and others.

Smaller, but not the Smallest

Small rabbits are in the range of four to seven pounds at maturity, or about 2.5 to 3 pounds when weaned. Many members of these breeds make really excellent pets because they are large enough to be held and

petted but are not too big to lift and carry when they become adults. The Dutch rabbit, which has markings reminiscent of those of the

Rex. Members of this breed, averaging nine pounds, fall into the medium-weight group of rabbits.

A White Beveren, another of the medium-sized rabbits.

Marked similar to the Himalayan, the Californian is over twice as large as the rabbit its coloring resembles.

panda, is a fine representative of this weight class. Others include the Tan, the English Spot, the Florida White and the Mini-Lop.

The Tiny Ones

The smallest rabbits include the Netherland Dwarf, which has so many

varieties, the Polish, the Holland Lop and the Britannia Petite. Many Netherland Dwarfs are found in pet stores. They are distinguished from the other tiny rabbits by their apple-round heads, very short ears and compact bodies. Also, they ordinarily have better dispositions than Polish and Petites, both of which are known to nip a handler on occasion. Dwarfs, Polish, Holland Lops and Petites weigh two to three pounds when adults and as little as a

pound or so when weaned. Holland Lops are, basically, Dwarf lop-eared rabbits.

FUR TYPES

Normal

Rabbits are also distinguishable by fur type. Most (36 of the forty breeds) pet rabbits have what is known as "normal" fur. Normal fur occurs in every weight class and looks basically the same on a Flemish Giant as it does on a Netherland Dwarf. It is about an inch long and quickly returns to its normal position when stroked toward the rabbit's head. The underfur is fine, soft and dense. Actually, the fur does more to make the rabbit so huggable and pettable than anything else. When normal fur is looking its best, usually during the coldest part of the year, it is said to have good "flyback," meaning it returns rapidly to its normal position when stroked the other way.

Rex

Rex fur is found on Rex rabbits only. Rex rabbits

hairs on normal-furred rabbits) are no longer than the undercoat. Some people will tell you that Rex rabbits have no guard hairs, but if you look closely you will see they are there. Rex fur is only about five-eighths of an inch long. There are people who say it looks like velvet.

Satin

Satin fur is found in rabbits so far only on the Satin breed, but attempts are probably being made to Satinize other breeds. Satins are very popular and come in the following colors: black, blue, choco-late, copper, red and white, and also in chinchilla, Californian and Siamese. All varieties of this breed are in the me-dium-weight class. Satin fur is character-ized by a small-diameter hair shaft and a more transparent hair shell than is dis-played by the normal-furred breeds. This greater transpar-ency of the outer

The Tan, one of the smaller breeds of rabbit, gets its name from its tan undercolor. (Not all rabbits are as relaxed while being held as this one is.)

are noted for their lovely fur. Breeders are working to produce Rex rabbits in a number of sizes; there is no giant Rex yet, but there is now a mini-Rex. Rex fur is short and plushlike. It stands upright, and its guard hairs (the long, top

A Netherland Dwarf. The fur type of members of this breed is categorized as normal: it is about an inch in length, with a soft, dense undercoat.

27

hair shell gives the Satin fur more intense color and more luster compared to the normal-furred breeds, except for the

Tan, whose sheen is unsurpassed for some reason. Satin fur equals normal fur in length, about an inch.

Angora

The last type of rabbit fur is that of the Angora breeds; the fur of the Angora is more correctly called wool.

The Angora rabbit comes in several breeds, including the English and the French. The English is the smaller, weighing 5 to 7 pounds at maturity. The French weighs about 8 pounds. Both look much larger because of their long wool, which is two and one-half to three inches in length. English Angoras are readily distinguishable from the French because they have abundantly

fringed and tassled ears. Angora rabbits are raised commercially for their wool, which is spun alone or with lambs' wool to make the most elegant and warmest of woolen garments. Mittens, hats and sweaters come readily to mind, but Angora wool is also used to make underwear for mountain climbers and skiers. Because it takes a year to obtain a single pound of wool from one Angora rabbit, the wool and the garments from which it is made are extremely expensive. Fifty-dollar mittens and two hundred dollar sweaters are not uncommon.

Angora rabbits are gorgeous when sporting a full growth of well-brushed and combed wool. But if you obtain an Angora rabbit, be prepared to be the one who does the brushing and combing. It can be very time-consuming and can be a chore or a labor of love, depending upon your point of view. Many persons who would like to raise rabbits for profit but who loathe the thought of having their pets eaten or used in medical research are attracted to the idea of raising Angoras, for they are merely shorn or plucked seasonally until they die of old age. The hobby of spinning and the skill of knitting, in combination with the raising of Angoras, can result in a profitable sideline occupation that can be carried out completely in the home.

AVAILABILITY AND SUITABILITY

Nobody will deny that people fall for a pet because of the way it looks to them, so the photographs in this book probably will mean more than anything else (except a real live introduction in the store) when it comes to the final choice of a rabbit as your pet. You didn't ask, but my first choice of a pet rabbit is the Dutch, and a male if possible. The male usually has a better disposition and makes a better pet.

Making the Selection

But let's get down to the individual choice. You have decided on the breed or at least the group of rabbits in the store from which you will choose your pet. What should you look for? What should you watch out for?

First, select a rabbit that looks well fed and hops about animatedly. Avoid one that huddles in a corner of the pen away from the others. Look for an

Dimes is the picture of contentment while being cuddled by the author's daughter Alyssa.

Signs of good health in a rabbit include bright, clear eyes, a clean, dry nose and fur that is uniform in appearance, i.e., without bare spots or sores.

inquisitive rabbit with bright eyes and a dry nose. Check the insides of the forelegs. If they are matted (the fur stuck together), it's a sign the rabbit has or recently had a cold. Rabbits with colds tend to wipe their noses with the inside of their front paws and legs.

Second, check its front teeth. The uppers and lowers should come together evenly, or mesh. If the uppers and lowers overlap significantly, the rabbit has malocclusion or "buck teeth" or "wolf teeth." Because rabbits' teeth grow continuously and must be ground down constantly by chewing, they must meet evenly. Otherwise they will continue to grow and prevent the rabbit from eating, causing its eventual death by starvation (unless they are periodically clipped with wire cutting pliers). Malocclusion ordinarily is a congenital defect, although some rabbits will pull their teeth out of alignment by chewing on their cages.

Third, make sure the rabbit is not suffering from diarrhea. Check the area around the hindquarters to make sure the fur is dry, clean and not matted. A perfectly healthy rabbit is perfectly clean, so there shouldn't be any excrement or stain of feces on it. A healthy rabbit's droppings are dry and hard. Accept only a perfectly clean rabbit. Because well raised rabbits are brought up in cages with wire mesh floors, even the bottoms of their feet should be perfectly clean.

Fourth, the ears should be checked. Look down inside them to make certain there are no crusty brown scales that would indicate ear mites. If the ears are clean (and assuming that the rabbit meets the other primary criteria), pick out a male if you can,

Ideally, a rabbit's upper and lower teeth should come together evenly, as shown here.

Siamese-colored Dwarf. After you select that very special rabbit, you will want to take every measure to ensure your pet's well-being and safety. Outdoor romps should take place only in enclosed areas.

because a male, or "buck," makes a better pet than a female, or "doe," which often may not have as sunny a disposition.

But male or female, health and vitality and cleanliness are most important. Don't buy yourself trouble and, perhaps, heartbreak.

Feeding

If you are like most other people you are convinced that you absolutely know— believe it. But the facts are quite different.

Nutritionists, those

A good diet will be reflected in the quality of your pet's fur. Pictured is a Himalayan, which is a small, sleek breed of rabbit.

and have incontrovertible evidence to prove—exactly what rabbits eat. Cabbage · and lettuce and carrots and plenty of them. Right? Sorry, friend, wrong. W-r-o-n-g. WRONG!

The popular notion, nourished by Peter Rabbit in Mr. MacGregor's garden, and Bugs Bunny, with the ever-present carrot that smacks of a gangster's cigar, would have you

professionals educated and trained to know better than anyone else exactly just what the nutritional requirements of various animals are, see it differently. They understand that the nutritional requirements of the domesticated rabbit reach protein, fat and fiber levels that the storybook and cartoon comestibles cannot meet. Just as human nutritionists, with their basic seven food groups, have determined what humans should eat, livestock nutritionists have concluded that rabbits require a balanced diet to grow and reproduce. There are plenty of things that a rabbit (and small boys, too) *will* eat, including what Peter and Bugs enjoy, but if you want your pet rabbit to be healthy and happy, you should feed him what he *should* eat. His nutritional future is in your hands. You are responsible for his health and well-being. And the foundation of that well-being is the food that you feed him.

I could offer you a chart that shows protein, fat, carbohydrate and fiber requirements, and you might shudder to think it's up to you to formulate the feed ingredients

Prepared rabbit food (or pellets) is the most important part of your pet's diet--not such foodstuffs as carrots and lettuce.

your rabbit requires to live and grow. But relax, it's easy. It's easy because it's all been done for you by those nutritionists I mentioned. And it's really a cinch to feed rabbits correctly, because *all* they really need to eat is contained in a single marvelous unit called the rabbit pellet.

Years ago it was a difficult task to feed rabbits properly. You had to search to gather all the feed grains and the roots and roughage (hay) that rabbits need. But now all the ingredients have been assembled and sacked up for you in the form of the bite-size rabbit pellet.

Your pet store should have rabbit pellets in stock. If you have only one rabbit pet, and perhaps a small allowance to buy feed, it makes sense to buy a few fresh pounds at a time from your pet store. Besides, it's a good place to visit regularly. You never know what's new. On the other hand, if you have a lot of rabbits, it is more economical to buy larger quantities at a feed and grain store. It really comes down to how much you need. But if you have only one pet rabbit, your pet store is your best bet.

Here's what these pellets contain:
• Alfalfa hay for high-quality roughage.
• Special sources of protein, including some of animal origin.
• Phosphorus, calcium, essential trace minerals.
• Sources of necessary vitamins.

Protein levels of these pellets range from 16 to 20 percent, the higher number necessary for the growing young rabbit, the lower needed as a "maintenance" diet for the adult rabbit.

The list sounds like something on a breakfast cereal box—you know, you've read it many times. But go back and read it again—especially the pro-

A rabbit's dietary requirements are quite simple. Your local pet shop can provide you with a nutritionally complete rabbit food for your pet.

35

tein levels—and you will see why the rabbit pellet outperforms your favorite cereal and is, in fact, a complete food for your rabbit.

The protein content and the ingredients of different brands of pellets may vary slightly; in fact, the contents of the same brand may vary depending on which feed mill produced it. But all the brands and the output of all the mills are good, and one thing, something I have repeated countless times and must say again, is certain: *If all you ever give your rabbit is pellets to eat and clean water to drink, you and he will be doing fine.*

Yet in spite of all the evidence that pellets are the best feed for rabbits, there are those who insist upon feeding them other things. That's when they get into trouble and when their rabbits get sick. And die.

Of course, rabbits can exist and even thrive on other feeds, although the odds are they won't. You might think you could feed a rabbit for less than pellets cost, but how much have you saved if your rabbit dies?

The price of pellets varies from maker to maker and seller to seller, and it varies also from one period of time to another, of course.

A Florida White awaiting mealtime. The hopper-type feeder is preferred by many hobbyists because the food can be put in from the outside of the cage without opening the door.

It also varies according to the quantities in which you purchase them; the larger the quantity, the less the cost per pound. But when you con- sider that the adult rabbit of the medium- weight breed range consumes only about four to five ounces a day, your cost is not going to be very great in any event.

This could run you more during the first few months you have your rab- bit, as he grows to maturity. If you have a young rabbit, less than six months old (or less than his mature weight if you don't know his age for cer- tain), give him all the rabbit pellets he will clean up in one day. By no means let any feed remain in the dish and get stale (let alone moldy). But make sure this young, growing animal gets all he can put away. You may also give some good dry hay (not green grass or clippings from lawns that have been treated with herbicides or

insecticides). You may provide all the hay your rabbit wants. My first choice is alfalfa, but just about any good, dry, leafy, fine-stemmed hay will do. Pet stores often sell alfalfa hay cubes, a very handy form to feed that rabbits enjoy.

Never give any greens—

An alfalfa hay cube is a good, nutritious snack for a rabbit. Items such as these can be purchased from your pet shop.

37

A Black English Spot. Food consumption varies with each individual rabbit. It is you who can best determine what your pet's needs are.

carrots, lettuce, cabbage or the like—to rabbits less than five or six months of age under any circumstances. They won't do a bit of good and can, of course, kill your pet. It's the drastic diet change that does it. Consistency is the key word. Rabbit pellets are consistent, because they contain everything the rabbit needs in every single pellet.

Adult rabbits of the medium-weight group eat about five ounces per day; again, more or less, depending upon the individual. A rabbit the size of a Dutch, for example, which at maturity is only half the size of a medium-weight rabbit, will consume only two to three ounces a day and cost you only half as much to feed, perhaps no more than thirty cents a week, no strain on even the most meager allowance.

But, you may ask, how much precisely should I feed my rabbit to make sure he gets enough but not too much (you don't want him too fat). There is no exact answer, but there is some precise advice. Keep a close watch on your rabbit, particularly at feeding time. Run your hand over your rabbit. If he's a bit bony, give him more. If he hasn't cleaned up his pellets, you are probably giving too much, so feed less. If he gets less than four or five

As you feed a young, growing rabbit all the rabbit pellets he can eat in a day, you will soon find out how much that is. A lot depends on the size and age of your rabbit. If he leaves some pellets uneaten, give less on the following day. If your rabbit greets you at feeding time by trying to tear the door off his cage to get at your feed sack, you will want to give him more.

ounces per day and he's a medium-size rabbit, something may be wrong if he doesn't eat it all up.

The first thing to check when you find that your rabbit is not eating enough is his water supply. Does he have a water bottle (we will cover watering equipment soon); if he does, is it working properly? Is the stem plugged? A rabbit that is thirsty will not eat dry rabbit pellets. He needs water at all times.

Second, note his droppings. They should be large and dry and round—well formed. This is a good time to watch out for diarrhea. If a rabbit is not eating well but otherwise is apparently healthy, try tempting him with a tidbit of dry bread, a spoonful of oatmeal or a piece of hard, dry cookie. Later on we'll talk a little more about potential problems

and their solutions. But these are just a few ways to get your rabbit back to the feeder.

FEEDING SCHEDULE

Never forget that when you cage a rabbit he depends on you. You eat every day. So does he. Even if you have to depend on others to prepare your meals, you can still find

How much your pet eats a day will depend upon his size and age.

In addition to food products, your pet shop also stocks various bedding materials.

and obtain a snack in between if you are hungry. Even the smallest child can crack the security net that surrounds the cookie jar. But a rabbit in a cage is completely at your mercy. If there is one thing a rabbit pet can teach you it is responsibility for a caged living thing.

So you never want to forget to feed your rabbit every day and at the same time every day. Rabbit keepers have known for years what farmers have done for years: feed their livestock before they sit down to their own evening meals. Think about it a minute: could you enjoy your own dinner knowing your pet rabbit is still waiting for his?

Besides, evening is the best time of day to feed rabbits. Sure, you could feed yours at

A Black Silver Fox doe. It is not difficult at all to keep your pet as healthy looking as this rabbit appears.

almost any other time of day, *regularly* each day, but evening is best, because rabbits are more active then than during the daylight hours. If you would like to feed your rabbit twice a day, divide the pellets into evening and morning feedings. But one feeding a day is enough.

Be sure to provide fresh water every day. This means dumping out any left from yesterday, rinsing the dish or bottle daily and washing and disinfecting it weekly.

So far I've suggested rabbit pellets and hay and water only. Later on I will in fact cover some other feeds to offer your pet as a *supplement* to the pellets. In the meantime, there often is the question of salt. Salt spools are for sale in pet stores, so they must be necessary, right?

Not really. If you feed rabbit pellets, they already contain salt. Additional salt in the form of a salt spool won't hurt your rabbit, but it might hurt the house you call his home. If the rabbit has a hutch with a wire mesh floor, the condensation and drip from a salt spool can rust a hole right through the bottom. Because salt is already in the pellets, there really is no need for it. If you insist on offering your rabbit salt, I'd salt his pellets in the feeder with a table shaker. At least that way you will save the hutch floor.

You might also ask about vitamins. Vitamin

A Netherland Dwarf. These little fellows—averaging two pounds at adulthood—will consume less food than their larger relatives.

41

Feeding

A White Flemish Giant *(right)*.

A Black Silver Fox *(below)*. Keep your rabbit away from any strange plant. It may be poisonous or may cause allergies.

supplements are available, often in liquid or tablet form. Because rabbit pellets are a complete food, they include vitamins and thus additional vitamins are rarely, if ever, called for.

Housing and Equipment for Your Pet

You picked out a good healthy rabbit and are feeding him correctly, but he's still in the box in the garage or basement, the most temporary and unsatisfactory of quarters. He needs a permanent home, and it's up to you to provide it.

First, suppress the carpentry instinct. Put away hammer and saw. Forget about boards and nails. What a rabbit needs is what he can't gnaw. And a rabbit can gnaw wood. A wooden hutch absolutely will not do. There is only one kind of hutch for your

Rabbits are clean animals, and their keeper should provide them with quarters that make it easy to keep them clean.

Rabbits on the loose are subject to worm infestation and can be attacked by hawks and other predators.

rabbit, no matter where you live, no matter what the climate. That is the all-wire hutch. You can build it yourself or buy it from the pet store. Compared to any other hutch you can build or buy, the all-wire hutch is superior. Consider no other kind. Outdoors, it will need protection from the weather, and some carpentry is required to build a protective shell for the hutch, but no carpentry is needed for the hutch itself. Indoors, it is fine the way it is.

Think of the following when considering a home for your rabbit. He needs clean quarters. He needs light and ventilation and protection from winds and drafts. He can take plenty of cold, but he cannot stand extremes of heat without suffering. He can't stand dampness—certainly not a wet floor. He does not need a whole lot of room; unlike their wild cousins, domesticated rabbits are not used to hopping great distances.

Next, think of yourself, the pet owner. You want to keep your pet safe from predators such as dogs or cats. You want to prevent escape—you don't want to lose your pet. You want ease of maintenance—this hutch should be easy to clean, because cleanliness is so important to the well-being of your pet. Self-cleaning is the ideal. The hutch must be easy to handle, adaptable for inside or outside use. It must be durable. It must allow you to feed and water your rabbit conveniently, if possible without opening the door. You must be able to see inside at all times. What good is a pet you can't see? Besides, it is the observant pet rabbit owner whose pet rabbit thrives. Your hutch must allow you

to reach and pick up your rabbit with ease. And it

should be inexpensive to buy or easy to build.

What we have just discussed is the all-wire hutch. Its most important feature is the floor, which is self-cleaning. Only an occasional wire brushing plus periodic disinfecting is needed. Droppings and urine pass right through to

A water bottle such as this is ideal for your pet. Its design prevents cage occupants from soiling their drinking water.

45

Housing and Equipment for Your Pet

A wire cage is your best bet if you want durable, low-maintenance housing for your rabbit.

the ground or a box or tray that can be emptied easily. It affords complete ventilation. It can accommodate a hopper feeder which requires none of the floor space and which you can fill from the outside. With this hutch you can use a water bottle or a water crock, which you can fill from the outside by pouring water into it right through the wire wall.

This hutch will last for years, because your rabbit can't eat it. And years from now, unlike a wooden hutch which will be soaked with urine and gnawed to nothingness, your all-wire hutch will still be serviceable. It will outlive your pet and be there for the rabbit who follows, or it will be worth selling to another pet owner for, most likely, more money than its original cost.

If I seem to go on and on about the all-wire hutch, relax, I'm about to quit. But I started housing pet rabbits in 1948, and I haven't seen anything in all these years to beat it. In spite of its attributes, however, I still see many

pet rabbits housed in smelly wooden crate cages, and this kind of housing has done more to give pet rabbits a bad reputation than anything else. It is housing such as this that makes some people say that

rabbits smell bad or even— you should pardon the word—stink. In fact, however, while manure or urine may smell bad, rabbits don't. They are very clean animals; they groom and wash themselves fastidiously. And it is a hutch that keeps them free of their waste that keeps them odor-free.

More and more pet stores sell wire hutches these days. If they don't stock them, they can order one for you. Feed stores surely will have them. If you can't obtain one locally, you could send away and order one through the mail. Or you can make one yourself. Plans are available.

Using The All-Wire Hutch Outdoors

To use the all-wire hutch outdoors, you need to provide some protection. The basic type of superstructure that is needed is similar to a tall table, but with a pitched roof to shed the rain. Four legs and a roof are all that is needed in warm climates, but storm curtains, perhaps of canvas or vinyl, should be available. Plywood or other types of paneling could be used on the sides. In colder climates, solid walls on the sides and the back of this slant-topped "table" will be required during winter months.

The height of this structure depends somewhat on the height of the rabbit keeper. It should be tall enough so that you don't have to stoop to see or care for your rabbit. But it shouldn't be so high that you can't see or reach inside. If you build this structure with a roof that overhangs the front about eighteen inches or two feet,

Many rabbit hobbyists use the manure that collects under the hutches as garden fertilizer.

A French Lop.

A section of the author's rabbitry.

it will provide shade and shelter from a slanting rain, and it will allow you, the owner, to take refuge from rain while you feed and water your pet.

If you use your hutch outdoors, you will have to provide protection from roaming dogs or cats. A sturdy fence, at least four feet high, all around your rabbit's home will ensure his safety. The importance of such a fence cannot be overstressed. Cats may try to nip your rabbit's feet or tail from under the hutch. Dogs may try to push in its door. They may simply frighten the rabbit to death, actually, by jumping up against the hutch. A frightened rabbit can panic and race wildly around its cage, perhaps injuring itself against a wall or water crock or even dying from exhaustion or heart seizure. So if there is the slightest possibility that dogs or cats or other dangerous-to-rabbits animals can get into the area of your rabbit hutch, a fence is required.

To use the hutch inside a garage, barn, shed or porch is an easy matter. You could provide legs (some come with them) to support it, or you could suspend it by wires. A metal pan or a wooden box lined with polyethylene will catch the droppings, which can be used in the garden.

Used inside or out, the hutch should be easily detachable from its super-structure or its legs. You will want to remove it to the back yard for an occasional hosing down and disinfecting. Sponging it off, after it is washed, with a liquid household disinfectant and then rinsing off the disinfectant (which probably is a poison), is a simple matter.

Another reason to detach the hutch is for greater enjoyment of your pet. With a lightweight all-wire hutch for a home, your rabbit pet can travel. He could go on vacation or spend the afternoon with you in the back yard of a friend. Or you could put it down on your own lawn on a sunny afternoon, where your rabbit could be your companion while you indulge in pleasant outdoor activities.

Other Equipment

You need either a feed crock, which your pet store has available, or a hopper feeder, which is probably also featured for sale in the store. The crock should be heavy crockery, not plastic. If it's plastic your rabbit will eat the dish for dessert. He will also tip it over and waste the feed. Investing in a good heavy crock for feed will pay dividends in saved feed. The best ones have a "lip" inside at the top to prevent the rabbit from scratching the feed out and wasting it.

A hopper feeder is made of galvanized iron. You fasten it to the front of the hutch, which lets you feed your rabbit without opening the hutch door. If you use a hopper feeder, you should not fill it up, but measure the correct amount of pellets for your pet and pour them in. If you must be away for a weekend, a hopper feeder allows you to put in extra feed, which descends from the hopper to the trough section as your rabbit eats. It is a feature that makes the hopper feeder my number one choice.

The size of your pet will determine the area of housing that you will provide. The Polish, pictured here, can do with a smaller living space than, for example, a Checkered Giant.

A Dwarf Lop. This kind of rabbit is very manageable and can make a fine pet.

First choice for watering equipment in warm weather (above freezing temperatures) is the plastic water bottle with the stainless steel stem. These are widely available and should be in your pet store. Get

narrower than the top on the *inside*. That way if the water freezes, the ice will slide *up*. You know that water expands when it freezes, so if the ice has nowhere to go but against the walls of the crock, you

the large size, which holds about a quart. On a hot day, your pet rabbit will be able to almost empty it. The water bottle is ideal because you put the water in and seal it up. The water stays clean. Also, it takes up no space on the hutch floor.

Of course, the bottle won't work when temperatures fall below freezing. That's the time to use a water crock or a metal water pan.

If you use a crock, be sure to examine the inside of it carefully before you buy. The bottom should be

will wind up with a broken crock. Again, avoid plastic—the rabbit will eat it. A metal pan is useful in the winter, because when the water freezes you can smack the pan on the ground and pop the ice out. Or you might simply dip the pan (or your crock) into a pail of warm water to thaw it and slip the ice out.

Water your rabbit twice a day or even more often if you can during freezing weather. A rabbit will not thrive if all he has for water is ice to lick.

It is convenient during cold weather to be the

A Tortoiseshell English Spot, bred and exhibited in Great Britain.

A Chinchilla.

owner of two watering crocks or pans. You keep one inside where it's warm to thaw. That way at watering time you don't have the problem of frozen crocks.

With some ingenuity and the expenditure of a little money, you can avoid the problem of frozen water. Immersion heaters such as are used in bird baths may be utilized. Or electric heat tape could be wrapped around your water crock, as long as the tape is protected from gnawing. You could electrocute your rabbit if you don't do this right.

Should Your Rabbit Run Loose?

Certain questions are going to arise sooner or later after you get your rabbit. Can you let him loose in the house or yard? Could he even be paper-trained or kitty-box trained or totally housebroken?

The answer to all of these questions is yes, but keep some other considerations in mind. First, this is an animal that gnaws. He can eat the furniture. Imagine what a gnawing rabbit could do to the leg

him a cold or
even pneumo-
nia.

Letting him
run loose in the
yard also has its
hazards. If your
yard is fenced in
or if you train your
rabbit to stay in it, you
aren't likely to lose him. He
must be trained enough,
however, to let you pick
him up whenever you
want. If he runs away
when you go after him, you
may never catch him. So
the first thing to do would
be to make him receptive to
your handling in a confined
area where you can catch
him. This might be the
fenced area around an
outdoor hutch. Repeated
experiences of being let
loose and picked up in
such an environment will
train him for the day you
let him run loose in your
yard.

of a Queen Anne chair.
This may not go over too
big in some households.

He can also eat electric
cords, such as for lamps
and appliances. One false
bite and you could be
needing a new rabbit.
Again, electrocution. The
best advice is to keep your
rabbit in his cage and out
of the house. If you must
bring him in and let him
run around on the floor,
make sure you are there to
supervise. Also, don't bring
him in from the cold during
the winter to play in the
warm house and then put
him back outdoors in the
cold. He can stand all the
cold temperatures you
have, but extreme *changes*
of temperature could give

If you do let him loose,
there are the usual dog
and cat hazards, but there
also are those of eating
something poisonous.
Right off, do not let a baby
rabbit (under six
months) run
around
on a
lawn
where
he can
eat the
green

grass. It can give him diarrhea and kill him. An adult rabbit will be okay if he nibbles a bit of green grass, provided you let him have just a little and don't let him mow the whole lawn. You have to make sure the lawn has not been sprayed or otherwise treated with chemicals against the invasion of weeds or insects, or your rabbit can be poisoned. Also, certain plants are poisonous. Rhododendrons, for example, and certain other trees and shrubs are poisonous if eaten in varying quantities. Again, you have to know the yard and you have to keep a close eye on things for the protection of your pet.

Protection From Extremes in the Weather

Before we end our discussion on housing and equipment, let's address the question of additional

Alyssa Bennett and Dimes provide each other with some warmth on a cold winter day. Rabbits do not mind the cold, but it isn't a good idea to bring them indoors in cold weather and then put them out again. The drastic temperature change could cause a cold.

protection for your pet against extremes of weather.

In the winter, you may want to provide additional warmth for your rabbit if his hutch is either ing fingers of young children—is to provide him with a box of shavings or straw to retire to when it's to his advantage. You could construct a wooden box about a foot by a foot and a half in floor area, with outdoors or in an unheated outbuilding. You might spread clean straw on his floor; if you do, the straw will need changing regularly. You might give him a board to sit on to take his feet off the cold wire. This is a pretty good idea.

Another good idea if your rabbit needs additional protection from the cold—or perhaps needs to be able to get away from the pokwalls about a foot high, and with either no top or perhaps a board over half of the top, to jump up to and sit on. You would cut a hole in the side of this box for the rabbit to enter. And you should drill some holes in the bottom, perhaps a quarter inch in diameter, for drainage. If this box fits easily through the door of the hutch you can take it out regularly for cleaning and to provide fresh shavings or straw or other suitable bedding, such as leaves (that are not poisonous), pine needles, ground corn cobs, peanut shells, bagasse (shredded sugar cane) or whatever other bedding material is available locally and suitable for such use. Your pet store personnel should be able to advise you, and they probably have bedding for sale. The main thing to remember is that your wire hutch is self-cleaning, but the wooden box is not. Also, keep in mind that dampness can lead to colds or other ailments, so keep it dry. If it isn't dry, it will defeat the whole purpose anyway, because a damp box is no refuge in cold weather.

Also, keep in mind that rabbits, being fur-bearing animals that grow thicker coats in winter, do not mind the cold. If you keep them out of drafts and keep them safe

from rain and snow, you will be giving them all the protection from the cold that they really need.

When it comes to extremes of heat, however, there is another story to tell. You should keep your rabbit shaded from the direct rays of the summer sun, and if you live in a very hot climate, a double roof, which allows air to circulate, or a heavily insulated roof is ideal. If your rabbit gets so hot (and the temperature would have to be above 90 degrees F. if you have your hutch shaded) that it begins to get wet around the nose and mouth, you will have to cool him down. To avoid this situation in the first place, you might put a plastic milk jug, perhaps the gallon size, filled with ice inside the hutch. You might have

A Siamese Sable. This breed is distinguished by the attractive lustre of its fur.

two of these jugs, one kept in the freezer compartment of your refrigerator and one in the hutch. When the one outside melts, replace it. The hot rabbit will lie against this jug, and the ice will keep him cool. Don't worry about his eating the plastic jug. If he does, you really didn't need it in there—he wasn't too hot to eat. To cool off a really hot rabbit in a hurry (but not *too* fast), wrap him in a towel that has been soaked in ice water and wrung out, or surround him with two or more jugs of ice. Put him down at ground level and

A White English Angora. Regular grooming is recommended to keep this breed looking its best.

in the coolest place you know. If you have a basement, it is probably cool, so take him down there. In fact, you might even want to move him in there during a heat wave. If so, his all-wire hutch is portable.

What About Toys?

When you are not giving him any attention, what's a rabbit to do all day? Nibbling hay is fine, and lying around doing nothing has its good points too. But sometimes a rabbit wants something to do.

produce a whole lot of it, but there are some important things you can do with rabbit manure. You can use it in a compost heap, for one thing. You may know that compost is really the rotted remains of any number of vegetable-matter items. Weeds, hay, leaves, vegetable peelings and tops—all these things can go into a compost heap. You could add eggs shells and other garbage (but not meat scraps), and if you pile it all up and wait long enough it all decomposes into what really looks like potting soil. It's really rich stuff that can be used in planting with great success. But to make it all really "work" and decompose at a fast rate, it needs an *activator*. One such activator is rabbit manure. If you mix your rabbit manure into the family compost heap, you will make the whole mixture decompose faster and become richer. Furthermore, when

If you provide a rabbit with a couple of small tin cans, such as frozen orange juice concentrate cans, he will just delight in tossing them and rolling them around. A stick or a branch (especially from a fruit tree) can be very appealing. A box to hop on or over is fun.

A Rabbit and a Garden

Gardening is the number one hobby in the United States. Millions of people are raising vegetables and flowers and shrubs. A rabbit can contribute to this garden, and a garden can pay him back.

Early in the book we briefly discussed the use of rabbit manure in the garden. Your rabbit won't

Although rabbits are generally considered gregarious animals, it is always best to house them singly.

A Sable Marten Netherland Dwarf.

you put rabbit manure into a compost heap, you are sure to attract earthworms. Earthworms will digest the whole pile, and their waste, or castings, becomes the most valuable part of the heap, because it has the most fertilizer value. Of course, attracting earthworms has another benefit if you or another member of the family or a friend like to go fishing.

One way or another, into the compost heap or directly into the garden, rabbit manure is a real contributor. If you have only a small amount and want to use it for best effect, dig it in around a rose bush.

Now, how can the garden contribute to the rabbit? Well, there are some food items that you can get out of it. You are probably wondering why I'd mention such a thing after all this talk about rabbit pellets. But if you have read this far, you know that rabbit pellets are the foundation of your rabbit's diet, so now I can tell you, the serious reader, that you may supplement these pellets with certain items from the garden.

The garden can help your rabbit most in the winter. That, of course, is when the garden has gone to bed for the year. But when the cold weather arrives and your rabbit's water freezes with some regularity, he will welcome some *roots* left over from the garden. Perhaps you may have kept some carrots or rutabagas or beets in a plastic bag in the bottom of the refrigerator. You can feed small pieces of these roots during the time your rabbit's water is likely to freeze. That way he gets some welcome moisture in his diet. Feed them only in small pieces and only to an adult rabbit. You don't have to limit them to the winter, but you will get the most benefit from them at that time of year. Remember to use them sparingly, and never give them to immature rabbits.

Handling and Health Care

Much of the enjoyment of having a pet rabbit is being able to pick him up, pet him, hold him and carry him about. There are ways of going about it that both you and he will appreciate.

First, think of yourself. Rabbits have sharp toe-nails, especially young rabbits. And they shed their fur on occasion. Furthermore, while they are usually very careful, sometimes a rabbit can have an accident while you are holding him, and your clothing might suffer.

So it's a good idea to have a long-sleeved shirt, smock or jacket made of a good sturdy material to

A healthy rabbit has bright eyes and a sleek coat; a healthy rabbit is alert and energetic.

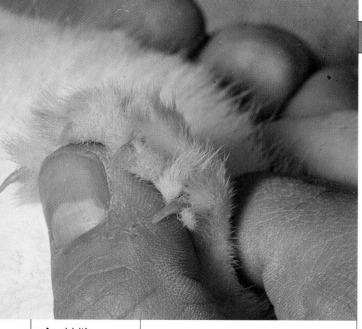

A rabbit's toenails are quite sharp.

Lifting a rabbit correctly.

long garment.

Next, think of your pet. Picking him up and playing with him should be an enjoyable experience for him. You certainly don't want to injure him. There are several ways to pick up rabbits, and some ways have to be avoided.

The main thing to keep in mind is to pick up the rabbit in such a way that he feels comfortable and secure. Never pick him up by the ears, and always support him under either the hindquarters or the chest (not the stomach) or both. If he feels comfortable and secure, he will not struggle or kick and scratch. Of course, if he kicks or scratches, that's

wear when you are handling a rabbit. Rabbit judges, who evaluate hundreds of rabbits at shows, usually wear a denim or twill jacket, sometimes even a "shop coat" type of

no fun for either of you. So take some time to look these photos over carefully.

Potential Problems

The first thing you ought to know about your rabbit is that you can't catch anything from it, with one exception. That's ringworm, which is caused by a parasite and is indicated by circular patches of fur falling out. It hardly ever occurs, but if it does, keep your hands off your rabbit and either contact your veterinarian or ask at the pet store for a liquid medication that can be applied. As I said, it isn't likely to happen, and it's easy to remedy—and it is the only ailment you could ever get from your rabbit.

Mothers are the first ones to ask about this sort of thing. They don't seem to care half as much what the rabbit can get as they do about what you might get from the rabbit. So they can rest easy. Rabbits don't need any shots, and they don't get rabies or distemper. From a health standpoint, it's tough to beat a rabbit.

When you selected your rabbit, you chose one that was healthy and active, if you followed my instructions. And if you are housing

Always support your pet's hindquarters when you lift him up.

A safe, secure handling technique.

No, carrots do not comprise a major portion of a rabbit's diet! Much more important is prepared--nutritionally complete--rabbit food.

and feeding your rabbit in accordance with the practices described in this book, you will be avoiding a lot of problems. But sometimes problems occur despite your best efforts. What we are going to do in this section is to talk about avoiding those that we can and solving those that we can't.

First of all, remember, a rabbit is a living thing. Every living thing is going to die some time. That's the way it is, and medical science hasn't been able to do a thing about it, when you really come right down to it. Rabbits live eight to ten years or more. I knew one that lived to be thirteen, and perhaps they live longer than that, but one day your rabbit is going to die. In the meantime, you want it in the best of health.

It's impossible to anticipate all the problems that can occur. If after consulting this book and others you may have you cannot solve a problem of health, then you must contact your veterinarian. But that will only be in very rare cases, I believe, if you have started with a healthy rabbit.

Let's talk about the kind of problems that *you* might cause, and how to avoid or solve them.

You might house more than one rabbit to a cage. That is not advisable, because if they are mature rabbits and they are both males they will fight, if they are both females they may fight, and if one is a female and the other is a male they may love, in which case you will wind up with a blessed event that you are not planning for. This can only mean disaster. A mother rabbit needs extra feed and a nesting box, and

she needs her *own* hutch. If baby rabbits are born in a hutch that contains another adult rabbit, the mother may not care for the young; she may even kill them. So the first thing to remember is that every

adult rabbit needs its own hutch. You may ask if rabbits get lonely and I may answer that I don't know. But I do know this: two adult rabbits (or more) in one hutch is asking for a problem. And we are trying to avoid problems.

Here's how to avoid some more:

• Maintain a regular feeding schedule with

If you would like to take your rabbit outdoors, a harness can be a very useful (and very safe) device.

works properly.

• If your rabbit isn't eating, first check the water supply.

• Keep a close eye on your rabbit. Check for the bright eye, the glossy coat; feel for the firm flesh and make sure your rabbit is active.

• If your rabbit is a thumper (like the rabbit in *Bambi*) give him a board to stomp on. The wire might hurt his feet. Check for sore feet if he stomps habitually.

• Watch the droppings. They should be large, round and firm.

• Watch for a runny nose or sneezing, which indicates a cold. Matted fur on the inside of front paws means your rabbit has a cold and has been wiping a runny nose.

Preventive Medicine

Your pet store may carry sulfaquinoxaline sodium. If it doesn't, your local feed and grain store does. If you can't find it locally, you can send away for it by writing to a supplier listed in a rabbit magazine. Sulfaquinoxaline sodium comes in a bottle. A pint of the concentrate, which should last for about a year, is very inexpensive. What it does is prevent coccidiosis.

Coccidiosis is the most

Checking for ear mites *(above)*.

Check your pet regularly to determine whether the flesh is properly firm *(below)*.

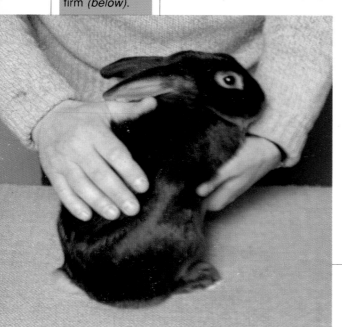

rabbit pellets. Never give greens to young rabbits.

• Keep the water fresh and pure. Rinse crocks and bottles daily, wash and disinfect weekly. If you use a bottle, make sure it

common infection of domestic rabbits; it can retard growth or even kill young rabbits. Diarrhea, bloated belly and generally poor condition indicated by a lack of gloss and general roughness of the fur are symptoms. A parasite causes coccidiosis. Sulfaquinoxaline sodium controls it. Directions come with the drug, but usually it is diluted with drinking water and given for two days in a row, withheld for two days and given for two more days, on a monthly basis. It's a regular treatment used by many rabbit raisers, and it prevents coccidiosis. I recommend you get a bottle and use it regularly.

If your rabbit has diarrhea, withhold its water and administer an anti-diarrhetic. This type of product can be obtained at your local pet store. Administer a dosage according to the weight of your rabbit. In fact, remember that most medicine is administered by weight. You're a mammal, I'm a mammal, elephants are mammals and so are rabbits. We all weigh varying amounts, and if you take that into consideration, you will be able to calculate dosages. Body weight is important.

Your rabbit should not develop ear mites if you keep it in a wire cage. Ear mites are parasites. Before they find a host, they live in manure. If your rabbit is in a wire cage, he does not come into contact with the manure and thus does not contract ear mites. I haven't had a case of ear mites in my own rabbits

Above: A healthy trio of youngsters.

since 1948, when I built my first cages with a wire floor. But you might get a rabbit with ear mites, or you might not take my advice about wire cages and your rabbit could get them. If so, it's easy to cure. You will note scabby encrustations inside the ears. Simply pour in a little mineral oil or even salad oil and you will drown them. It might take a couple of applications. Put in about half a teaspoonful. An eye or nose dropper is a good applicator.

Another problem that occasionally occurs in rabbits is sore hocks. If a rabbit's hind foot or feet become ulcerated, perhaps from stomping on the cage floor, we call that sore hocks. First, give him a resting board to get his feet off the wire

An eyedropper is very useful for administering medication in the ears.

floor. Mild cases can be treated with iodine or an antibiotic ointment if you can get your hands on one. If the condition persists, take the rabbit to your veterinarian. When you pick up your rabbit each day, look him over, including his feet. Your sharp eye and daily vigilance will help you spot small problems before they get to be big ones.

These are a few of the problems that can plague your pet rabbit. They aren't likely to, but they might. Some other problems may not really be big problems in themselves, but they can be seen as such by family

A Sable Marten. Check your pet daily for any abnormalities, such as sores or bald spcts.

A young White New Zealand.

and neighbors.

One is flies. If flies surround your rabbit hutch, remove the manure regularly from under the cage. Flies breed in manure; if the manure isn't there, they won't be either. If family or neighbors spot a few flies, they may cause you a problem. So make sure you don't have any. If you can't remove the manure regularly to a compost heap or the garden (nobody will complain about flies in the garden, for some reason), dust under the hutch with limestone, the granulated or powdered kind sold in garden supply centers. You can buy a fifty-pound bag for a relatively small sum, and it ought to last you a couple of summers. You won't have the problem, of course, during cold weather.

Another is mice. Nobody wants mice around. You won't have any if you feed your rabbits only the amount of feed they can eat in a day and keep the pellet supply in a metal container with a tight lid. If you leave a bag of pellets lying around outdoors or in the garage, you will attract mice. And mice can be a problem.

I don't know of another animal species so problem-free. There are some other problems that rabbits

Rabbits will gnaw on various and sundry items, so use discretion when permitting your pet to be out of his cage.

can have, but they are not common and really not worth going into. Don't forget to ask the pet store personnel about problems, and ask them to recommend a veterinarian if you don't know one.

I guess I should leave you with one other thought. I have pointed out that you are responsible for this animal. And if you are conscientious, as I hope you are, you will not take any responsibilities lightly. I'm dead serious about mine.

But, remember, if you are conscientious, and if you have one rabbit pet, you may think you have problems when you really don't. So if you think there is something wrong with your rabbit, ask another person to look him over before you become overly concerned. Animal problems are not terribly different from species to species. Ask an experienced dog or

cat owner, or the keeper of a guinea pig. Find another rabbit owner and compare notes. Ask the pet store people who else has rabbits. Ask your friends who

A Dutch Black.

Rabbits are remarkably free from some of the diseases that plague other kinds of animals.

has rabbits. Tell people you have one. That way they will tell you about others who do. It's comforting to have someone to ask and to tell your troubles to. Often enough, the trouble's over in the telling. A sym-pathetic and experienced ear is all that's needed to solve many a problem.

A Netherland Dwarf. If you want to let your rabbit outdoors, it is vital that he be supervised at all times.

70

Rabbit Shows

A beautiful rabbit begs to go on display, and it would be a shame if nobody saw him but you and a few friends who happen to visit. You could put him on display—in fact, even in a rabbit show.

About one thousand rabbit shows take place in the United States each year. Rabbit fanciers in the United Kingdom and several other European countries also conduct rabbit shows.

In the United States alone in the early 1980s, there were some 350 local and state specialty rabbit clubs. That figure has risen significantly over the past decade. Additionally, state rabbit associations (some states have several), national clubs, youth clubs, and fairs that get involved in rabbit shows have enjoyed a marked increase in participation by rabbit fanciers of all ages.

But you may never have read about one of these shows in the local paper. As a participant activity,

A prize-winning English Angora. The heavy tassels on the tips of the ears are characteristic of the breed.

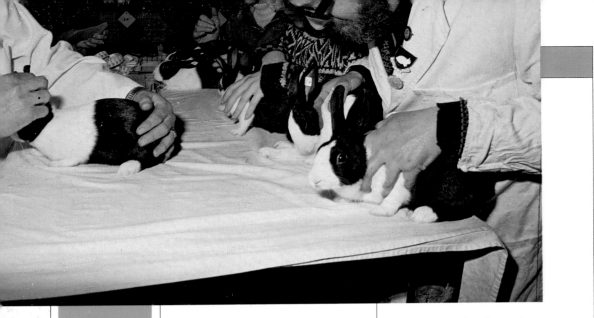

Dutch rabbits competing in an English rabbit show.

A Harlequin Rex.

rather than a spectator sport, it's rare that rabbit shows get publicity except in rabbit publications.

Shows generally take place in the spring and the fall. Summer is often too hot and travel too uncertain in many locales.

To find out everything you need to know about an upcoming show, you need to get the *show catalog*, which is nothing like you would receive from a large mail-order merchant, but instead is a modest (often mimeographed and stapled) description and set of instructions regarding entry, including an entry blank.

One way to locate a show is to ask your pet store manager. Very likely he will know about shows and can put you in touch with the right people. If he can't help, you could contact your local 4-H office, the county extension agent, your closest agricultural college, headquarters of the closest agricultural society or county or state fair association. If all that fails, you can write to the American Rabbit Breeders Association, P.O. Box 426, Bloomington, Illinois 61702.

You have to get the show catalog in advance of the show, not only so you can plan your day, but also because entries must be sent in to the show secretary in advance. Most shows have a modest entry fee per rabbit, and most of that money goes to pay the judge.

Rabbit shows can be divided into two types, basically. The first is just for fun. It's a pet show where rabbits are shown against other pets, including dogs and cats and birds and fish. Or it might be just against other rabbits, but still only for fun. Such shows usually are organized by playgrounds, recreation clubs and even the 4-H. Any kind of a rabbit, whether purebred or of doubtful ancestry, is welcome at this kind of show.

More serious rabbit shows are those sponsored by one of the rabbit associations mentioned above and sanctioned by the American Rabbit Breeders Association (in the United States and Canada) or other breed associations in other countries. In such shows only purebreds

Creme D'Argent.

A judge examining a Chinchilla at a show.

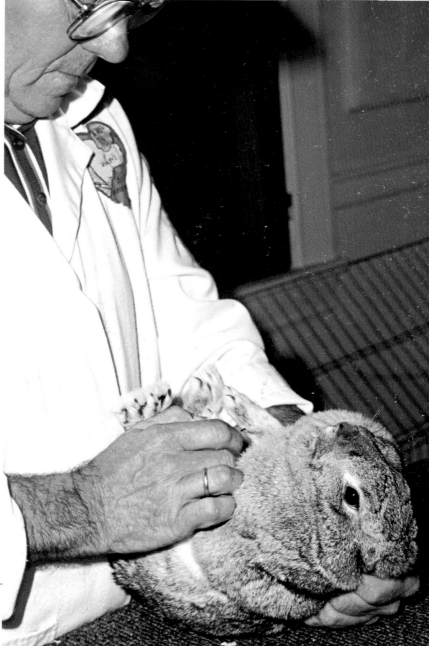

Award-winning Chocolate Tan.

Netherland Dwarfs at a British rabbit show.

have a chance to win, because each breed is judged separately by a judge who not only compares all of the rabbits present but also is totally familiar with the *standard* for each breed. The standard is a written physical description of the ideal specimen of each recognized breed, giving size, shape, color, weight and other specifications, right

down to the color of the toenails.

Whole books have been written about rabbit shows, but it should be enough to say here that it can be a lot of fun for the entire family. Many people combine shows with sight-seeing, picnics and even fishing trips. At the show, there is the chance to meet other rabbit owners and to talk about caring for your pet. Probably most important, however, even more than the money and trophies or ribbons you can win, is getting the judge's opinion and making your own comparison of your rabbit to those others you will find at the show.

What should you do to get your rabbit ready for the show? You should be keeping your pet in top condition all year long. Proper and regular feeding and watering and clean living quarters will ensure that your rabbit is looking his best. Perhaps a few minutes a day spent brushing him with a soft bristle brush will give his coat extra sheen. You might try that for a week or two before the show.

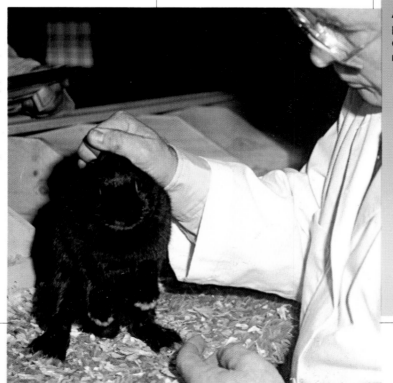

A judge preparing to examine a rabbit.

A Smoke Pearl Marten Netherland Dwarf.

Mating and Raising Rabbits

Rabbits are prolific breeders. Pictured: a Lop.

Many persons are involved in mating and raising rabbits today because they once had a single rabbit for a pet. If one can be so much fun, how much better it would be to have many—that was the thought that occurred. And it can be fun and an interesting and even profitable hobby to raise rabbits if you are in the right circumstances and the right frame of mind.

One rabbit is easy and fun to take care of. Several rabbits can complicate your life. Each adult rabbit must have its own hutch. Do you have space for more than one hutch? Baby rabbits can stay with their mother for perhaps

An 11-day-old Tan.

Dwarf Lop buck. For some fanciers, the most exciting part of their hobby is raising new stock.

they sell or give away young rabbits as pets to others the offspring will not only two to three months. After that, each of them will need its own hutch. Because litter sizes can number six to eight or even more, can you picture as many as a dozen rabbit hutches at your house? Will you have the space and the time and the money for that many rabbits and their equipment? Or will you be able to limit yourself to, perhaps, a pair of breeders and then dispose of the youngsters when they are old enough to leave? This means you must find some way to give away or sell the rabbits. Emotionally, some people have a difficult time with this. For example, they are concerned that if

receive the kind of care they ought to get. Once your baby rabbits leave you, you can't stop little children from squeezing them too hard or perhaps forgetting to feed and water them. So it isn't just finding a way to dispose of the rabbits, it's coming to grips with the conditions they will find themselves in after they leave your care. There is a continuing demand for most kinds of rabbits for use as highly wholesome and digestible meat, but many pet rabbit raisers cannot stomach that idea. Therefore, before you decide it would be fun to raise a litter of baby rabbits, give some long, serious thought to the consequences of such an action. Remember that rabbits are prolific, and any rabbit raiser who is successful at raising them must also be successful at disposing of them.

If you do give all of the foregoing a lot of consideration and decide to go ahead and raise rabbits anyway, give the whole idea a little *more* thought. If you are going to produce some young rabbits that you plan to part with, why not determine ahead of time where they are going to go, and for what purpose, and then produce the kind that will be most acceptable in the market-place.

That means choosing a breed to produce that somebody else wants, not just what you like. If, for example, you are going to produce meat rabbits, you need a breed bigger than the Dwarfs. Laboratory rabbit buyers usually want white rabbits—so think about New Zealands or White Satins or Florida Whites. Pet buyers will want rabbits as attractive as yours—so perhaps producing more of what you now have is the thing to do. The thing to do, that is, if you have a purebred rabbit to start with. If you have a pair of mongrels, there's really no telling what you will get when you mate them. If your pet rabbit is a mongrel, you may want to exclude him from a mating program. Perhaps now is a good time to discuss this a little further.

A purebred rabbit is one bred to a certain written physical description, or *standard*. Such an animal is sometimes also called a *thoroughbred* and it may even be termed *pedigreed*. Someone else may call it

Selecting a suitable pair for mating is of special importance if you intend to breed good specimens.

79

registered. Here's how to discuss those terms, including *mongrel*, or *crossbreed*.

A red-eyed White Holland Lop.

It should be pretty clear that a mongrel, or crossbreed, has unknown ancestry. Clear, because the rabbit looks like no other you have ever seen, or clear because there is no *written record* of its ancestry. A so-called mongrel or crossbreed rabbit *may* in fact be a purebred or thoroughbred (for our pur-

poses, these two terms are synonymous), but if there is no written record, nobody knows for sure.

This written record, or pedigree, should show three generations behind the rabbit in question—the parents, the grandparents and the great-grandparents. If you have a rabbit with such a record of its heritage, you have a pedigreed rabbit, but *not necessarily* a purebred. If indeed all the ancestors shown on this written record, or pedigree, are of the *same breed*, you are the possessor of a purebred or thoroughbred that happens to be pedigreed. It is possible, however, to carefully record the ancestry of a mongrel, showing the various ancestors of various breeds. Such a specimen is thus pedigreed, but it's still a mongrel.

A registered rabbit is something else. If a *purebred*, *pedigreed* rabbit is owned by a member of the American Rabbit Breeders Association, he may have it examined by a licensed ARBA registrar. That registrar, upon examining the rabbit and its pedigree, *may* recommend it for registration. The owner must send the registration application, along with a fee, to ARBA headquarters. If it is accepted, the rabbit will be considered registered and granted a registration certificate. No rabbit thus is registered until it receives such an examination and passes it, and no rabbit under the age of six months may be so examined. So no baby rabbit is ever registered. No rabbits are born registered. They must be examined and pass the test. If they do,

registration signifies that they meet the *minimum* requirements for members of that breed, as described in the standard. How do they pass the test? The registrar ascertains that they resemble, right down to the color of the toenails, the description written in the *standard*. If three generations of rabbits are registered, they are said to be registered *red, white*

Consider carrots a supplemental "treat," and not a substitute for pellets.

81

and blue. Should you buy a rabbit that is registered red, white and blue, you have a rabbit with formidable credentials. But why should you even consider such a thing? What significance is there, how important is it, for a rabbit to be registered? To the producer of rabbits for either pets, breeding stock, laboratory or meat purposes, registration is proof of purebred stock that meets the minimum requirements of the breed. Registered rabbits generally are the best available, even though registration makes pets no friendlier, meat no tastier. A breeder who begins with registered rabbits or their offspring can be reasonably certain he is beginning to mate and produce good rabbits, because every rabbit is really no more than the sum of its forebears.

And remember this about pedigreed rabbits, or even registered rabbits. If you don't get the papers with it, the rabbit is not, for all practical purposes, pedigreed or registered, no matter how pure its breeding actually may be, no matter that it passed the registrar's test with flying colors. Without the papers, you can't prove a thing, and the rabbit is worth considerably less.

Mating the First Pair

While all it takes to produce rabbits is a buck and a doe, if you really plan to raise rabbits, I suggest starting with four—two bucks and two does. I wouldn't try to build a herd from

two or even the well known "trio" of two does and a

Remember that a successful breeding program requires space, time, and money.

A red-eyed White Netherland Dwarf with her young.

A small litter is not profitable for a commercial breeder.

will be able to sell and breed from pairs and trios from two different litters from four different parents; such offspring are usually more desirable than a brother-sister pair. You might want to read up on genetics in general, and there are several books available on animal breeding. The principles of genetics are basically the same, no matter which mammal species you deal with, and what you read about dogs or cattle will apply to rabbits.

If you have a dwarf-sized or small breed of rabbit you should not mate them until they are five months of age. The medium breeds

buck.

The reason for this suggestion is that you probably will want to keep open the option of selling some breeding stock yourself, and you will want to start yourself off with a fairly broad base for further breeding. With two bucks and two does, you

least two feet by two and one-half feet floor space.

For the moment, you don't need a nest box, where the litter will be born, but you do need to keep track of what you are doing so that you will know when to put the nest box in and when the litter will be born.

The best way to keep track is with a doe's *breeding card*. Such a card is easily made, or you might find some free ones in the pet store or a feed store or at a rabbit show. The card you make could be of the three inches by five inches variety. It should

should be six months and the giants should be nine months. You can see that the smaller breeds mature sooner than the larger ones.

Your doe will need a hutch that contains as many square feet of floor space as she weighs in pounds. Therefore, if your doe is, for example, a New Zealand White that tips the scales at 10 pounds, you will need a hutch of about 10 square feet. A Dutch or Tan-sized doe, which matures at about five pounds, requires five square feet of space. The Tan does in my rabbitry have hutches of at

A Britannia Petite.

Genitalia of a male rabbit.

growls and resists the buck's advances, she *may* be pregnant. If she accepts the buck, you will want to record the date. You must observe the first date, but if she does not "kindle," as rabbit raisers call giving birth, you will want to respect the second date. But we are getting ahead of ourselves a bit.

include the following information: her birth date, her name or number if you have given her one and the names of her sire and dam (father and mother) if you know them. With this information you know when she's old enough to mate and which buck to select for mating if you have more than one available.

When you mate the doe, you write in the name of the buck and mark the date of "service," or mating. Testing is an unpredictable process, but if you test your doe for pregnancy, mark the date under a category called "tested." One way to test for pregnancy is to return her to the buck's hutch about two weeks after mating. If she

With the card on the hutch, you are ready to take the doe to the buck's hutch. Do *not* put the buck in with the doe, as a fight is sure to ensue. So remember to put her in his hutch.

Close the door and don't take your eyes off the pair; if you do, you might miss the whole thing. Rabbits have quite a reputation for breeding. If everything works right, it will be all over before the door swings shut. The buck will mount the doe. The doe will raise her rear end. The buck will service the doe and fall over backwards or on his side.

That's all there it to it, so take the doe out and put her back in her hutch, and be sure to mark the date of the service. Some rabbit raisers take her back for another mating about six to eight hours later. Doe rabbits are not known to have a cycle, or a time when they are fertile, but rather become fertile upon stimulation by the buck. It takes about six to eight hours for the eggs to descend and be fertilized by the sperm from the buck, and thus another mating often works very well to improve the chances for conception.

Sometimes, but not often, you might put the doe in with the buck and nothing will happen. The two of them just sit there. No mating takes place.

The first thing to do is make sure that you really have put a doe in with a buck. This may sound silly, but sometimes people are very surprised to find out that their boy is a girl and vice versa. Especially if, when they bought very young rabbits, they simply took somebody's word for it regarding the sex of the two. So take a look and see what you really have. In mature rabbits, the sex

Shown here are both ends of the color range in the self-colored Netherland Dwarf:

A Dutch. The Dutch pattern can be bred into many rabbit varieties and can be established in many colors.

organs are quite obviously distinctive. If you are not certain, pictures in this book should be of help.

Okay, you have a doe in with a buck but still nothing happens. If the buck is not interested, try another if you have one. If that's not the case, then here's a suggestion that works time and time again. Take the buck out of his hutch and put him in hers. Leave her in his. Let them stay in each other's hutch for a day or so—at least overnight. During this time they will acquire each other's scent, and the next day they are much more likely to be interested in mating. At that time, take the doe back to her own hutch, where the buck is waiting, and put her in.

You should be successful. If she runs away from him, gently holding her by the scruff of the neck (the loose skin over the shoulders) until he catches her and mounts her will help. Keep this in mind: sometimes a doe will run away and act as though she has no interest whatever in mating. But watch her tail. If she twitches her tail, you can be sure she simply is playing hard to get. She may run for awhile, but she will stop pretty soon. Never leave the pair unattended; you will never know whether a mating has occurred.

Once the doe has been mated and she's back in her hutch with the hutch card marked, you will want to keep an eye on the calendar, and if you have never waited for baby rabbits to be born, I can tell you two things: first, it takes thirty-one days, give or take a day; and second, it will be the longest thirty-one days you ever experienced. You will be waiting in eager anticipation.

During this waiting period, you should feed the doe her normal ration, no more than she gets ordinarily. There are a couple of reasons for this. In the first place, you really don't know that she actually is pregnant, and you don't want to overfeed her so that she gets so fat she won't be able to get pregnant in the future. That can happen. A doe can build up internal fat that sur-

temptation to feed her more. There will be plenty of time for that after the litter of baby rabbits is born.

On the twenty-seventh day after mating, as you consult your doe's breeding card, it is time to give her a nest box with nesting

Rabbits selected for breeding should be in top physical condition.

rounds the Fallopian tubes, through which the eggs descend to be fertilized, and choke off that descent, actually blocking the tubes. Second, an overly fat doe can have a problem in giving birth that can create a lot of physical stress and even, in extreme cases of obesity, kill her at kindling time. Resist the

material.

For medium-size does, this box should have a floor space of about twelve by eighteen inches. It should be about a foot high all the way around, except for about six inches high in the front, to permit her to jump in. For smaller sized rabbits, the box can be scaled down. Dutch and Tans, for example, can make do in a box about fourteen inches by ten inches. Dwarfs can use even smaller boxes, but those a little larger don't hurt.

The top of this box should be open, or you might have part of it enclosed, perhaps the back half. But it should be largely open, to provide plenty of ventilation. The bottom should have a few holes drilled in it for drainage. Avoid dampness in the box at all costs.

All-wire nest boxes with corrugated cardboard liners are available for sale and are my first choice. Wooden boxes can be easily made, however, from thin plywood or boards. Do not attempt to use a card-board nest box. In the first place, the doe will be able to tip it over, perhaps with fatal results for the litter. In the second, she will doubtless destroy it— actually eating it up.

If you live in a cold climate, this nest box will need a couple of inches or more of shavings or similar nesting material on the bottom. Fill it the rest of the way to the top with straw (not hay, which she will consume). The doe will burrow into the straw or shavings before the litter arrives. She will make a hollow, cylindrical nesting space inside and line it with fur she will pull from her own chest and stomach with her teeth.

After they are born, she

If you have to transport your rabbits, a carrying cage such as this will be very helpful to you.

will pull more fur and cover the litter. If she does a good job of this, the litter will survive in temperatures as cold as below zero. If the weather is warm, make sure you provide only a handful of straw on top of the shavings, to make sure the litter is not going to suffocate from the heat. Winter or summer, gauge the amount of nesting material by the temperature. But always make sure your box has good ventilation.

The litter probably will be born at night. This is a time when the doe needs peace and quiet. Resist the temptation to peek in and see whether the youngsters have arrived. This is a good time to provide her with a bit of green feed, such as a leaf of lettuce or a piece of carrot or apple. The doe usually is quite thirsty at kindling time, and she will appreciate this treat. Of course, you will want to make especially certain that she has plenty of fresh water to drink.

Keep any dogs or noisy children away at this time, if at no other. Peace and

A litter resting comfortably in the nest that the mother has lined with her own fur.

quiet are the key words.

The day *after* the litter is born, remove the nest box and take it out of sight of the doe. You should see the fluffy fur quivering with the young underneath. Carefully push the fur aside and—without touching the youngsters if possible—count them and remove and let nature take its course. Many will survive. Some breeders remove and destroy the runts immediately, figuring they may not survive, and if they do they will only be taking milk away from the others and that milk won't, ordinarily, make them anything but sub-par anyway. Cover all

Alyssa Bennett and Dimes, who is perfectly at home in his Easter basket. Raising a rabbit can be a very rewarding, enriching experience for a youngster.

any that might have died. You may find a runt that perhaps will survive or perhaps may not. I usually leave them with the mother the babies with the fur and replace the box where it was.

Now you will want to feed the doe all she can eat, and

I would make sure she has feed in front of her constantly. If you can spare some milk at this time, she will surely appreciate it. Powdered milk is very good. Tidbits of green feed, by which I mean *small* pieces of lettuce, carrot or apple (no cabbage) can be fed each day until the litter comes bounding out of the box, when you will want to cease with the green stuff, for fear that the youngsters will get hold of it.

In about ten days the babies will open their eyes and at about three weeks will be out of the box. In warm weather, you will want to remove the box at about three weeks to four, and in cold weather per-

haps keep it in another week or two. Be sure, during this time, that the box is clean and dry. This may mean dumping out the nesting material and putting in fresh shavings and straw. Of course, in warm weather, as the young rabbits grow rapidly and fur out completely, you will need very little nesting material other than a couple of inches of shavings.

Just before they come out of the box it's a good thing to disinfect the floor of the hutch (and to remember to rinse well after disinfecting).

As soon as the litter comes out of the box they will begin to eat the pellets, but they will still be nursing. Do not, of course, let them have any green feed

A lovely Harlequin. This is one of the more rare breeds of rabbit.

A Siamese Smoke Pearl Netherland Dwarf.

A Tri-color Rex. Note the unusual color pattern.

at all, but if you have some milk or dry bread they will relish it.

Keep pellets before them at all times.

Weaning Time

There is really nothing mysterious about weaning. It is simply the time when the youngsters start eating solid food alone and are separated from the doe. But it's a good idea to remove them from the doe a few at a time over a period of several days, to let the doe's milk dry up gradually. Take out the biggest and the huskiest first, letting the smaller ones stay for more milk.

If you wean the rabbits at eight weeks or so, you can let them stay together in another hutch for perhaps another month, but after that you will need separate hutches for each buck, or they will fight. Does may be left in one hutch for up to another month or so, but it's a good idea to provide each one its own hutch. Depending upon how and when you plan to dispose of the young rabbits,

you will have an extra month or two before you really run into a housing problem.

But, chances are, by then the rabbit will be somebody else's housing problem—or, more probably, another pet rabbit owner's new opportunity.

For Your Information

The two major national rabbit associations in English-speaking lands are the American Rabbit Breeders Association (P.O. Box 426, Bloomington, Illinois 61702) and the British Rabbit Council (Purfoy House, 7 Kirkgate, Newark, Nottingham, England).

National rabbit associations have much of value to offer to rabbit fanciers residing in their areas, and they should be contacted by anyone who wants to find out more about rabbit shows or who wants to obtain information about membership.

Index

A Siamese Smoke Pearl Netherland dwarf.

Index

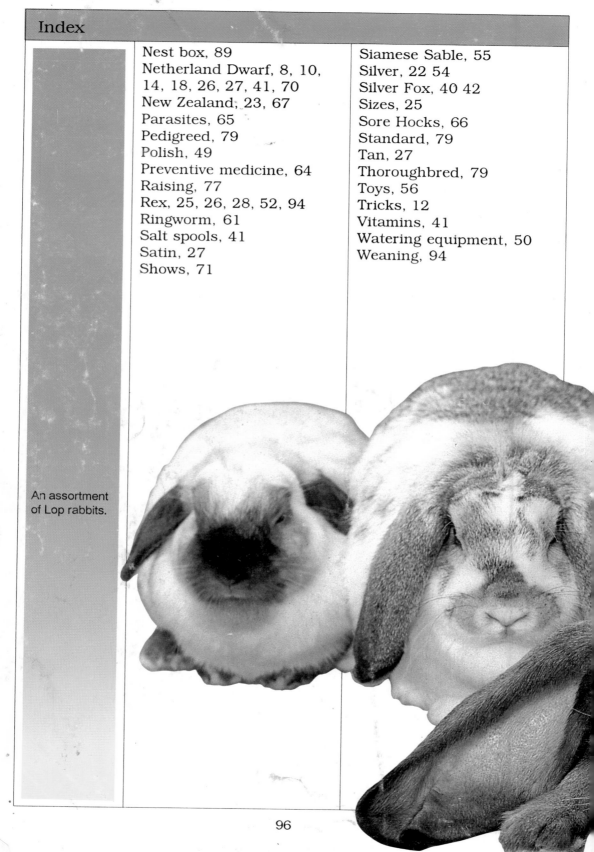

An assortment of Lop rabbits.